Countries of the World

Dominican Republic

by Muriel L. Dubois

Consultant:
Jeanne Marion-Landais
First Secretary
Dominican Embassy in Washington, D.C.

Bridgestone Books
an imprint of Capstone Press
Mankato, Minnesota

Bridgestone Books are published by Capstone Press
151 Good Counsel Drive, P.O. Box 669, Mankato, Minnesota 56002
http://www.capstone-press.com

Library of Congress Cataloging-in-Publication Data
Dubois, Muriel L.
    Dominican Republic/by Muriel L. Dubois.
    p. cm.—(Countries of the world)
    Includes bibliographical references (p. 24) and index.
    ISBN 0-7368-0812-4
    1. Dominican Republic—Juvenile literature. [1. Dominican Republic.] I. Title. II. Countries of
the world (Mankato, Minn.)
F1934.2 .D83 2001
972.93—dc21   00-009637

Summary: Introduces the geography, animals, food, and culture of the Dominican Republic.

Editorial Credits
Tom Adamson, editor; Karen Risch, product planning editor; Linda Clavel, production designer
    and illustrator; Katy Kudela, photo researcher

Photo Credits
Beryl Goldberg, 12
John Muldoon, cover, 10
L. Paul Mann/Mercury Press, 6, 8
Marshall Smith, 18
StockHaus Limited, 5 (top)
Suzanne Murphy-Larronde, 14, 20
Visuals Unlimited/Joe McDonald, 16

1 2 3 4 5 6 06 05 04 03 02 01

Table of Contents

Fast Facts

Name: Dominican Republic
Capital: Santo Domingo
Population: About 8.5 million
Language: Spanish
Religion: Mostly Roman Catholic

Size: 18,815 square miles
(48,730 square kilometers)
The Dominican Republic is about twice the size of the U.S. state of New Hampshire.
Crops: Sugarcane, coffee, cocoa

Maps

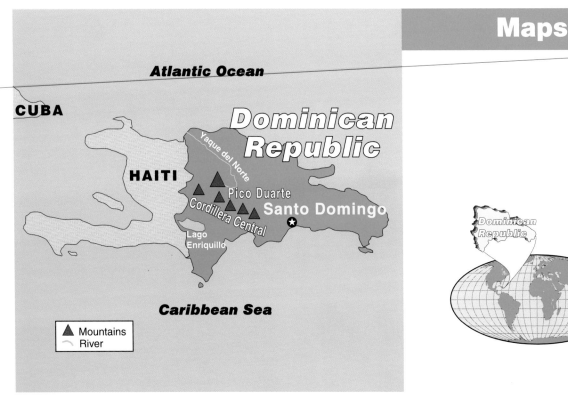

Atlantic Ocean

CUBA

Dominican Republic

HAITI

Yaque del Norte

Pico Duarte

Cordillera Central

Santo Domingo

Lago Enriquillo

Caribbean Sea

▲ Mountains
🌊 River

Dominican Republic

The flag of the Dominican Republic is red, white, and blue. Blue stands for the sky. Red is for the blood of those who died for freedom. White represents the light of the sun. A white cross divides the flag into four rectangles. The country's coat of arms is in the center of the cross. The coat of arms is a symbol of the country.

Currency

The unit of currency in the Dominican Republic is the peso. One hundred centavos equal one peso.

In 2000, about 16 Dominican pesos equaled 1 U.S. dollar. About 11 pesos equaled 1 Canadian dollar.

The Land

The Dominican Republic is the second largest country in the Caribbean region. Only Cuba is larger. The Dominican Republic covers about two-thirds of the island of Hispaniola. The country of Haiti covers the rest of the island.

Mountains, valleys, and beaches stretch across most of the Dominican Republic. The Cordillera Central mountain range rises near Haiti and nearly reaches the Caribbean Sea. The country's southern coast touches the Caribbean Sea. The northern coast meets the Atlantic Ocean.

The Dominican Republic has both the highest and lowest points in the Caribbean. Pico Duarte juts above the Cordillera Central. This mountain is 10,417 feet (3,175 meters) above sea level. Lago Enriquillo is near Pico Duarte. This saltwater lake is 144 feet (44 meters) below sea level.

The country's longest river is the Yaque del Norte. It is nearly 240 miles (390 kilometers) long.

The Dominican Republic has beaches along its coasts.

Life at Home

Family is important in the Dominican Republic. Family members form close bonds. When a man and woman marry, their families support each other.

Some Dominicans live on large farms. They grow crops such as coffee and sugarcane. Some farm owners live in large homes. Their workers might live in wooden houses or huts made of palm leaves and mud. Tin roofs keep out the rain. Floors are made of cement or dirt.

Housing can be hard to find in cities. Many people move to cities to find work. Some poor people live in small shacks. They make shelters from cardboard and other items they find. Wealthy people in cities live in large, modern homes.

Many people paint their homes with bright colors.

Going to School

Children in the Dominican Republic begin school at age 7. They are expected to attend school until at least eighth grade. Many families cannot afford books, paper, and pencils. Some children work to help their families instead of going to school. Other children care for younger brothers and sisters. Some children have no transportation to school.

More than half of all students attend the six-year liceo (lee-SAY-oh), or high school. Children do not have to go to school after they turn 14. Many students drop out because they cannot pay for their books.

The government is working to help students by rebuilding schools. Many public schools offer "desayuno escolar," or breakfast at school. This program encourages more students to attend school. Each year, more people in the Dominican Republic learn to read and write.

Students at some schools must wear uniforms.

Dominican Food

Plantains are an important food in the Dominican Republic. This fruit looks like a large banana. Plantains have thick skins and must be cooked before people can eat them. Fried plantains are called tostones. Boiled and mashed plantains are called mangú.

Dominicans eat more plantains, rice, and beans than they eat meat. They have a rice and bean dish named for their flag. White rice and red beans are part of la bandera. Bandera is the Spanish word for flag. The colors in this dish remind Dominicans of their flag.

Families try to eat meals together. If they can, parents leave work at midday. Lunch, called comida, is the main meal of the day. The family might eat sancocho (sahn-KOH-choh), a meat stew. After lunch, people take a siesta (see-ESS-tah), or nap. Supper is a light meal. Families eat lunch leftovers, snacks, or cooked eggs.

Plantains are larger than bananas.

The güira, accordion, and tambora are instruments used in merengue music.

Music and Dance

The merengue (muh-RENG-gay) is the national dance of the Dominican Republic. Its lively steps come from African and European dances.

Traditional merengue bands use four instruments. The accordion plays the melody. The tambora, güira, and marimba keep the beat. The tambora is a small drum. The güira is a metal cylinder that a musician scrapes with a metal stick. The marimba is a wooden box with metal keys that a musician plucks. Today, merengue bands also might use guitars or synthesizers.

Merengue dancers sometimes wear traditional clothing. Girls wear long, colorful dresses or skirts. Boys wear dark pants and a loose shirt called a chacabana.

Merengue songs cover different topics. They can be about love, nature, or problems in the country. Merengue songs sometimes are funny.

Animals

No large wild animals live on the island of Hispaniola. American alligators live in Lago Enriquillo. Bottlenose dolphins and manatees are native sea mammals.

More than 200 species of birds live throughout the country. Pink flamingos also make their homes near Lago Enriquillo. Parrots, pigeons, and nightingales fly through the forest. Pelicans, ducks, and spoonbills live near the sea.

Settlers brought the mongoose to the Dominican Republic from India. They wanted the mongooses to eat snakes and rodents. But they also ate birds and other animals.

The Dominican Republic has several endangered species. The American crocodile lives near lakes and rivers. The rhinoceros iguana and Ricord's iguana can be found in dry areas. The solenodon is about the size of a rat. This small mammal hunts for insects at night.

Rhino iguanas can be 2 to 4 feet (.6 to 1.2 meters) long.

Sports and Games

Baseball is the most popular sport in the Dominican Republic. U.S. Marines brought the game to Cuba. Cubans then brought it to the Dominican Republic.

Dominican boys start playing baseball when they are young. Baseball season begins in October and ends in February. Many Dominicans play professional baseball in the United States and Canada.

Many Dominicans enjoy golfing, fishing, and scuba diving. The Dominican Republic has many public and private golf courses. Deep-sea fishers catch marlin, sailfish, or tuna off the coast. Divers explore coral reefs. Soccer, basketball, and volleyball also are popular sports.

Dominoes is the most popular game in the Dominican Republic. People often play on tables outdoors. Families play at home. Children learn to play dominoes when they are young.

Baseball is popular in the Dominican Republic.

Holidays and Celebrations

Dominicans celebrate their independence on two days. February 27 is Independence Day. Dominicans honor the day in 1844 when they became free from Haitian rule. They enjoy parades and carnivals all over the country.

Spain took over the country in 1861. But the Dominican Republic fought and won independence from Spain on August 16, 1865. Dominicans celebrate Restoration Day each year on this date.

Lent is the 40 days before Easter. Dominicans celebrate Carnival during the weeks before Lent. During the final days of Carnival, people wear masks and costumes in the streets.

In 1492, Christopher Columbus and his crew became the first Europeans to land on Hispaniola. Some people honor each October 12 as "el día de las razas." They honor the time different races began mingling in the Americas.

Large, colorful masks are part of Carnival.

Hands On: Play Thumper

Thumper is a game from the Dominican Republic.

What You Need

6 or more players
A chair for each player

What You Do

1. Put the chairs in a circle so players face one another.
2. Each player picks a different hand signal such as snapping fingers, touching the nose, or pulling an ear lobe.
3. Choose one person to be the leader. The leader uses one hand to tap a rhythm on his or her leg.
4. Everyone follows the rhythm along with the leader.
5. The leader keeps the rhythm, performs his or her own hand signal, then someone else's.
6. The person whose hand signal is picked goes next. He or she performs his or her hand signal and someone else's. This player must keep tapping the rhythm.
7. Play continues until someone makes a mistake. A mistake might be forgetting a signal or missing the tapping rhythm.
8. The person who makes a mistake must pay a penalty picked by the group. A penalty is usually something silly: hopping around the circle on one foot, spelling your name backwards, or singing a song in a loud voice.
9. After the penalty is paid, start the game again.

Learn to Speak Spanish

yes	sí	(SEE)
no	no	(NOH)
mother	madre	(MAH-dray)
father	padre	(PAH-dray)
please	por favor	(POR fah-VOR)
thank you	gracias	(GRAH-see-ahss)
hello (good day)	buenos días	(BWAY-nohss DEE-ahss)
goodbye	adiós	(ah-dee-OHSS)

Words to Know

Christianity (kriss-chee-AN-uh-tee)—the religion based on the life and teachings of Jesus Christ

coat of arms (KOHT UHV ARMZ)—a design, usually in the shape of a shield, that stands for a family, city, or country

endangered species (en-DAYN-jurd SPEE-seez)—a type of plant or animal in danger of dying out

mammal (MAM-uhl)—a warm-blooded animal with a backbone

sea level (SEE LEV-uhl)—the average surface level of the world's oceans

synthesizer (SIN-thuh-sye-zur)—an electronic piano keyboard that can create sounds made by other instruments

traditional (truh-DISH-uh-nuhl)—using the styles, manners, and ways of the past

Read More

Creed, Alexander. *Dominican Republic*. Major World Nations.
Philadelphia: Chelsea House, 2000.

Rogers, Lura, and Barbara Radcliffe Rogers. *The Dominican Republic*.
Enchantment of the World. New York: Children's Press, 1999.

Useful Addresses and Internet Sites

Consulate of the Dominican Republic
10187 104th Street, Suite 100
Edmonton, AB T5J 0Z9
Canada

Embassy of the Dominican Republic
1715 22nd Street NW
Washington, DC 20008

The Embassy of the Dominican Republic
http://www.domrep.org
The World Factbook 2000—Dominican Republic
http://www.cia.gov/cia/publications/factbook/geos/dr.html

Index